For my great-grandmother Ana Elisa Hernández Aldamuy,
who came to America; for Pura Belpré, who preserved our stories;
and for my titi Rose, who inspired me to tell this one —A.A.D.

With all my love for my Ratón Pérez, Alejandro Mesa —P.E.

Special thanks to Pedro Juan Hernández and el Centro de Estudios Puertorriqueños

Planting Stories: The Life of Librarian and Storyteller Pura Belpré • Text copyright © 2019 by Anika Aldamuy Denise • Illustrations copyright © 2019 by Paola Escobar • All rights reserved. Printed in the United States of America. • No part of this book may be used or reproduced in any manner whatsoever without written permission except in the case of brief quotations embodied in critical articles and reviews. For information address HarperCollins Children's Books, a division of HarperCollins Publishers, 195 Broadway, New York, NY 10007. www.harpercollinschildrens.com • ISBN 978-0-06-274868-3 • The artist used Adobe Photoshop to create the digital illustrations for this book. • Design by Chelsea C. Donaldson • 18 19 20 21 22 PC 10 9 8 7 6 5 4 3 2 1 ❖ First Edition

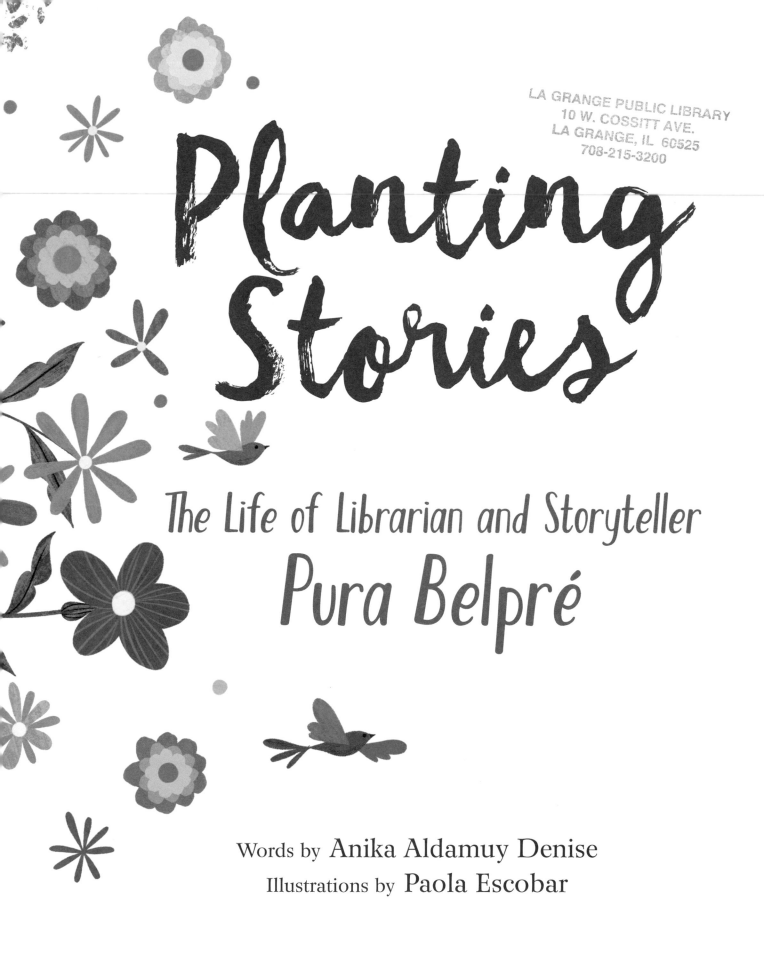

Planting Stories

The Life of Librarian and Storyteller
Pura Belpré

Words by Anika Aldamuy Denise

Illustrations by Paola Escobar

HARPER

An Imprint of HarperCollinsPublishers

It is 1921.

Pura Teresa Belpré leaves her home in San Juan
for a visit to Nueva York.
Words travel with her:
stories her abuela taught her.
Cuentos folklóricos Pura retold in the shade of a tamarind tree,
in Puerto Rico.

Now a new island stretches before her—
ripe for planting seeds of the cuentos she carries.

Manhattan.
A city of hustle and bustle.
Bigger, louder, crowded—
yet alive with hope and possibility.

What began as a visit to celebrate her sister's wedding
becomes the first steps in a new land—
y una vida nueva—for Pura.

She works first in a garment factory.
But it is cold floors and hard edges,
not the soft, fertile ground
where seeds take root.

Then—a golden opportunity! ¡Una bendición!
The library needs a bilingual assistant.
Pura speaks Spanish, English, and French.
She is perfect for the job.

But where are her abuela's stories?
Not one folktale from Puerto Rico is on the shelves.

How lucky for the library that Pura has story seeds ready to **plant and** *grow.*

In the children's room,
she lights the story hour candle . . .
and begins:

Her eyes dance!
Her voice sings!

Pura's words paint a picture
of a little house with a round balcony,
where Martina, a beautiful Spanish cockroach,
meets Pérez, a handsome and gallant mouse.
El ratoncito Pérez y la cucarachita Martina,
a tale from the tamarind tree.

When Pura's story is done,
each child makes a wish on the candle,
and, with a wisp of air . . .

whoosh!

La vela is blown out.

Now Pura has a wish, too:
to plant her story seeds throughout the land.
Pura learns to make puppets.
She snips and sews their clothes . . .
paints their delicate faces.

Families come
to hear folktales en inglés y español,
to watch Pura's puppets
dance across
the stage
of her stories.

But the library needs libros for its shelves.
How can more children read *Pérez y Martina*
and other cuentos de Puerto Rico?

Pura puts her story in an envelope
and mails it to Frederick Warne, a publisher.

Soon, *Pérez y Martina* is a book!
Now a published author, puppeteer, and storyteller,
Pura travels from branch to branch,
classroom to classroom,
to churches and community centers . . .
planting her story seeds
in the hearts and minds of children new to this island
who wish to remember
la lengua y los colores of home.

Writing, learning, speaking, teaching, traveling:
Pura does not slow down.
Until—

like the beautiful Martina,
she meets her Pérez.

On a December day in New York,
Pura marries the musician Clarence Cameron White.

Un año away from the library, she decides.
One year, to start a new life—as a wife.

Chuí

Chuí

Chuí

Chuí

But a year . . . stretches on.
Together, they travel to new cities.
Clarence plays his music.
Pura tells her stories.

They are happy years
of music and writing,
separations and reunions,
friends, family, and stories—
always.

Until on a June day in New York,
Clarence stops playing his music.
And Pura's story must begin again.

It is 1961.
Pura returns to the library.
There are others now,
storytellers
who make puppets dance,

who read *Pérez y Martina,*
The Tiger and the Rabbit, Juan
Bobo, The Three Magi,
and many more of Pura's stories
to the children.

The seeds she has planted,

the roots that grew shoots into
the open air of possibility,
have become a lush landscape
into which she steps, as though she has never left.

Author's Note

The seeds of the idea for this book first took root as I stood in the New York Public Library's central branch, gazing up at a large black-and-white photo of Pura Belpré: author, storyteller, and the first Puerto Rican librarian in New York City. Seeing the larger-than-life image of this remarkable boricua woman I'd long admired, I felt a swell of pride and, along with it, the warmth of recognition. For Pura's photo brought to mind my titis (aunts): first-generation mainland Americans whose parents migrated to New York from Puerto Rico.

Pura Teresa Belpré was born in 1899, in the rural town of Cidra, Puerto Rico, to a family of storytellers. Many of the folktales she learned as a child were told to her by her grandmother.

"I remember during school recess that some of us would gather under the shade of the tamarind tree," Pura wrote. "There we would take turns telling stories. These stories came with me to the United States. I thought of myself as a storyteller. I wished to be like Johnny Appleseed, who in the United States was known for planting apple seeds across the land. . . . And so I wished to plant my story seeds across the land."

But being like Johnny Appleseed was not always Pura's dream. She had planned on becoming a teacher and enrolled at the University of Puerto Rico, poised to begin her studies. Then, in 1921, she traveled to New York for her sister Elisa's wedding. She may have chosen to remain in New York simply because she liked it. Or perhaps, like many immigrants arriving in America, she was drawn by the promise of opportunity.

For Pura, opportunity arrived at the New York Public Library. After working briefly in the garment industry, Pura was hired as a bilingual assistant at the 135th Street branch, in Harlem. Her job was to find books and create programs that would appeal to the neighborhood's growing Spanish-speaking community.

When Pura discovered there weren't any actual Spanish books in the library, she wrote them herself. They became the first mainstream Latinx storybooks published in America. Putting to use the skills she'd been learning in library school, Pura made colorful puppets for bilingual story hours and hosted traditional Latinx holiday celebrations featuring folktales performed in English and Spanish.

Spanish-speaking immigrants who once thought the library wasn't for them now felt at home. Pura's boundless energy, curiosity, and captivating storytelling transformed the branches where she worked into vibrant cultural community hubs.

Even into her later years, Pura took buses and trains across the city, uptown and downtown, from the Bronx to the Lower East Side, bringing her magical storytelling and puppetry to children.

On the eve of her death on July 1, 1982, Pura received a Lifetime Achievement Award from the New York Public Library. Now each year the American Library Association recognizes outstanding works of literature by Latinx authors and illustrators with the Pura Belpré Award.

Her life and work as a librarian, storyteller, author, and advocate for the Latinx community is a testament to the power of our own stories to build bridges—not just to literacy, but to social change. Every time I enter the bright and cheerful children's room of a library or read a Puerto Rican folktale to my daughters, I think of Pura and feel grateful for the seeds she planted.

Selected Bibliography

Flores, Juan, ed. *Puerto Rican Arrival in New York: Narratives of the Migration, 1920–1950*. Princeton: Markus Wiener, 2005.

Matos-Rodríguez, Félix V., and Pedro Juan Hernández. *Pioneros: Puerto Ricans in New York City, 1896–1948, Bilingual Edition*. Charleston, SC: Arcadia, 2001.

Sánchez González, Lisa. *Boricua Literature: A Literary History of the Puerto Rican Diaspora*. New York: New York University Press, 2001.

Sánchez González, Lisa. *The Stories I Read to the Children: The Life and Writing of Pura Belpré, the Legendary Storyteller, Children's Author, and New York Public Librarian*. New York: Centro de Estudios Puertorriqueños, Hunter College, City University of New York, 2013.

Archival Collections

Clarence Cameron White Papers, Schomburg Center for Research in Black Culture, New York Public Library.

Pura Belpré Papers. Archives of the Puerto Rican Diaspora: Centro de Estudios Puertorriqueños, Hunter College, City University of New York.

Articles and Films

Aguiar, Eduardo, producer/director. *Pura Belpré: Storyteller*. New York: Centro de Estudios Puertorriqueños, Hunter College, City University of New York, 2011.

Jiménez-García, Marilisa. "Pura Belpré Lights the Storyteller's Candle: Reframing the Legacy of a Legend and What It Means for the Fields of Latino/a Studies and Children's Literature." *Centro Journal* 26.1 (Spring 2014): 110–47.

Further Reading

Engle, Margarita. *Bravo! Poems About Amazing Hispanics.*
Illustrated by Rafael López. New York: Henry Holt, 2017.

González, Lucía. *The Storyteller's Candle/La velita de los cuentos.*
Illustrated by Lulu Delacre. New York: Lee & Low, 2008.

Hood, Susan. *Shaking Things Up: 14 Young Women Who
Changed the World.* New York: HarperCollins, 2018.

Stories by Pura Belpré Mentioned in This Book

Pérez y Martina is about a beautiful and refined cockroach named Martina, and Pérez, a dashing mouse. The story begins with many suitors coming to Martina's balcony requesting her hand in marriage. One by one, she asks them: "How will you talk to me in the future?" Señor Cat answers, "Miaow, miaow, miaow!" Señor Duck says, "Quack, quack, quack, quack." Señor Cricket peeps, "Coquí, coquí, coquí." It is not until Señor Pérez wins her over with his lyrical "Chuí, chuí, chuí, chuí" that Martina agrees to marry him.

Juan Bobo is one of the most beloved folkloric characters on the island of Puerto Rico. He is typically portrayed as a trickster or a fool—and often both. In Pura Belpré's *Juan Bobo*, he dresses his mother's pig in fine clothing and leads her prized duck into a jug of molasses.

The Tiger and the Rabbit is a retelling of another classic folktale featuring a trickster: El Conejo (the Rabbit). Señor Tiger is always trying to catch Señor Rabbit and eat him, but the clever conejo outwits the hungry tiger again and again.

The Three Magi is a tale most often told near El Día de los Reyes (Three Kings' Day), a traditional holiday celebrated in Puerto Rico and other Hispanic countries throughout the world. On January 5, the eve of El Día de los Reyes, the Three Magi—King Gaspar, King Melchor, and King Baltazar—encounter difficulties on their way to bring presents to all the little children of Spain.